The Fulgent Requiem

william frank

TUCKFORD BUNNY PRESS

ISBN-13: 978-0-578-77057-4

Printed in the United States of America.
First Printing: November 11, 2021
Second Printing: February 19, 2023
Third Printing: February 14, 2024
Fourth Printing: January 17, 2026

For Scrambles

Other books by William Frank:

Slumgullion (2019)
The Purgatory Elm (2018)
Yuneko (2015)
Fiasco Galante (2014)
The Encolpia (2011)
The Morphine Fawn (2009)

All Tuckford Bunny books are available at Amazon.com and other retailers.

About Tuckford Bunny Press
Tuckford Bunny Press is a private, make-believe press that publishes the literary works of William Frank. It is the only make-believe company that will publish such funny-headed little books.

Acknowledgements

Floral designs on the Book's back cover and Title page used from the Permission-Free Designs in the book Art Nouveau Motifs, Dover Publications, Inc, Mineola, NY, 2002.

The cover photo was taken by the author on a trip to Rome in August, 2015 where he somehow yet again ended up in an alley and thus began his lifelong habit of riding his fiery bicycle without pants and bloomers.

The sigil of Zepar that appears in the poem, *The Chthonic Demotion of Malfeasance Mary Guttergung* appears in The Goetia, Clavicula Salomonis Regis, published by Samuel Weiser, Inc., York Beach, ME, 1995 and is used as part of the public domain.

The photo in the Top Story from the *Conspicuous Minister* is indeed the author, fist-bumping the world since 1970.

The Bear Photo preceding the poem *Ursine Industries*: Berserker Tableau is from a Hallmark Shoebox© card I purchased for my niece's birthday and in which I included that story, with love.

I am grateful to the editor of the now-defunct magazine *The Dillydoun Review* where "Uriah" first appeared online, in an earlier version. I have no proof it was published there, of course, since the site has been taken down and replaced by a page from a foreign power, which is a typical setback in my publishing career. You'll eventually have to trust me.

Tuckford Bunny Press *Loves its Fans*!

Dear Mr. Frank,

After setting myself on fire again attempting to firebomb your apartment, I feel compelled to write to you. While I admire you for your devious cunning and perseverance, as I have moved thirty-four times to escape you and am now living in an artificial cave I dug myself, at great expense and personal injury, I must demand you stop publishing your books immediately: Plagiarism is an ugly business but publishing my books word for word is criminal at best, desperate, shameless and mendaciously immoral at worst. The fact that you're publishing them first does not give you ownership of them or otherwise prove that you are their original and sole author. I call on you to stop mocking me and to desist from all surveillance of me at once. I must also take this opportunity to deride your ridiculous disguises, postures and voices, which also point up your total lack of creativity for which you obviously feel the need to steal other people's work. I know, too, that you are reading my mind and so I have now taken measures to thwart you, to the point that I have partially caved in my head, so don't even think about scanning me.

As I pursue a legal case against you, please know that if I find another book of my poems under your name, I will kill you.

Respectfully,
Flash Lampton

TUCKFORD BUNNY PRESS

Dear Flash Lampton,

We are very sorry to hear you were on fire and unwell. In the hopes we can aid a speedy recovery, we have enclosed two complimentary books, *The Purgatory Elm* and our latest, *The Fulgent Requiem*, both sure to dazzle, warm and entertain you!

We're sure that after reading these books, you'll want to explore all of our unique and magical titles! You can find us on the web at www.TuckfordBunnyPress.com or write to us to request our full catalog. We can ship anywhere in the world, with new express two-day shipping to shelters, prisons, asylums and caves so check us out today!

We know you have a lot of choices when it comes to books and we value your patronage. Thank you for your interest in our poetry, get well soon and *happy reading*!

From Your Friends at **Tuckford Bunny Press**

P.S.: Handsome Tuckford Bunny Press Bookmarks are now available for $1.95 each or ten for $10 (plus shipping and handling) when you use your very own personal coupon code *I Love TBP*. Order yours today!

Contents

About the Author:

William Frank, an author of seven books of poetry, is a man with an amiable façade, a witless disregard for reasonable care and a personal nimbus almost nine feet high. His work has previously appeared in the now defunct *The Dillydoun Review* and he was a runner-up for the 2008 *Discovery/The Boston Review* prize offered by the 92nd Street Y.

When not writing poetry, he enjoys long hours of losing at chess, bingeing on Japanese Cinema of the 40's, 50's and 60's, taking naps with Scrambles his cat, summering with the Devil, punching cryptids in the face and Kulning.

✿

"You are old, Father William," the young man said,
"And your hair has become very white;
And yet you incessantly stand on your head —
Do you think, at your age, it is right?"

"In my youth," Father William replied to his son,
"I feared it might injure the brain;
But, now that I'm perfectly sure I have none,
Why, I do it again and again."

~Lewis Carroll

✿

Doomsday in the Bayard Arboretum

Let's spread my blanket beneath this tree
        to make a checkered bed,
        the terrible creatures overhead,
with cheese for you, cherries for me.

Though everywhere's the end of days
        the fires, the suffering and the fear,
        I have sandwiches, your favorite beer
and, before forever, cold green grapes.

The Hearse with the Green Buckles

The Hearse is coming down Kickpuddle Lane
and I must be ready for it,
my cat in my arms, my flower pinned,
and my tears with my handkerchief.

The beautiful Hearse is on its way
to tell where the margin is lost,
as I look to the land where the moonlight is faded
and we change to the Hearse of the frost.

Sfumato the Marionette

The play closes with riotous applause
  when I endure the climactic scene
  under Miss Terry's Guillotine,
the satisfaction of all mother-in-laws.

Miss Terry's with the proper poppet now
  as my head pops off each night
  to the crowd's gross delight,
I chase it when I take a bow.

The Manager punches me in that head,
  the script girl says I got it wrong:
  I'm headless *after* I sing my song,
how can I sing after I'm dead?

I get one third of a third of the puppetmaster's pay.
  What do I care for the play's great tangle?
  I would rather drink coffee and dangle
at Max's Marionette café.

Prayer has made me bleary-eyed
  just like Max's stroppy waiter,
  prickly snaps as a gator...
maybe his girlfriend died.

Here, the deal is positively fatal
  when it comes *No Strings Attached.*
  What's today's catch?
I guess I'll have the special,

I say with a purple sigh.
  I've little rabbits round my belt,
  my pants are made of yellow felt,
Life sometimes makes me cry.

Tears are lanterns in the Grand Canal
  from suicides and lost loves,
  roses, letters, velvet gloves,
all the flotsam of former pals.

I watch in a daze as they drift by Max's.
  The sorrows tally, the Fates withhold
  from what dreams work in hope and gold
to pay Love's sad and lonely taxes.

Some like to play their fantasies straight,
  some like to swing on their affairs
  and some, like me, are Solitaires
who only play with twos and eights.

Some are edibly unhappy
  and so desperate for romance
  they'll far outdo the dance
in tangled puppetry.

Life again has let me down.
  My heartstrings wrinkle for Miss Terry
  a buxom maple girl, and very,
who lives in a suitcase *quite uptown.*

She is a spirited marionette.
  She clubbed me with a hot breadpan,
  and ran off with another man
just as far as her string would let.

But I guess that's just what you get
  when your head is made of wood,
  when you're not handsome or any good
at songs, poems or curvets.

Max, that wise old wood, agrees:
  Some has many and some has none,
  some are hapless and some are dumb
and the best isn't always for blocks like me.

O poor Max, do you ever close
  when sick or for the holidays?
  "We all have to jangle for our pay,
we all can't be in shows!"

When the play its dream each night breaks up
  the boys that star as the Riff Raff,
  no longer having to mug and laugh,
have their bitters in a cup.

All twenty of them at one table
  club together in a pile,
  I send a wave and a smile
they discard just like a Playbill.

The Professional Union of Ne'er-do-Wells
  meets here every Wednesday night
  but then attendance is always light
as quite expected of dumbbells.

As a member, I know too well
  the scrounging, listless, lonely times
  of anoraks, poets and archimimes.
I have a talent I cannot sell.

Off goes the bells in the wind-up clocks,
  the Factory empties to change shifts,
  I drink mine down and leave a tip,
I wander home back to my box.

I pass a sleepy delivery boy
  with his broken bike and a bruise,
  I buy the *Punch and Judy News*
who says they're closing the Viceroy

due to the theater's slumping sales.
  My head goes all the way around
  til I hear the amazed, delighted sound
of the child's bright and laughing gales.

Cinquain Between Our Houses

Homeward
At dawn from yours
Over our worn hill,
Longing following fragrantly
Like dill.

The Cricket Limerick

The moonlight shines on Tucket Hill,
and in the crickets' starry still
  the sleep is easy, the wine is sweet,
  we trill together in the heat
and no one misses us or will.

Nudist in the Cemetery of *Christina Mirabilis*

I like to dance through the cemetery on St. Christina's Day
wrapped only in the silence of good-byes,
a long disused hill where the only other stray
comes dusk and dawn to wear away my quiet.

What is vulgar here among the forlorn graves
to those naked to the bone beneath sweet grasses?
It's only when I return I'm sore ashamed
of breaking again my only pair of glasses.

Some prefer the beach to exalt their nakedness
while in the park the Adamites undress
as the joggers bounce past in the nude, running

to raise money for cancer; perineum sunning,
the *Soleil Society* points their toes to the sky
but I prefer the graveyard; don't ask why.

The Beautiful Park at Weltschmerz

Our moon is drawn across by sables,
   sound out the triumph on golden horns,
dress rich foods out on the tables
   and shovel the flowers across the lawns,

   let each morning the landscape change,
the Seasons break at once to sing
   til the winter is mad and the summer is strange
and the autumn shows corals like spring,

where Balloonists wander above the park
   and cats, wrapped like loaves of bread,
watch from cuddles a boy at the cart
   eat a pretzel as big as his head,

   while poets row their yellow punts
down the dandelion streams
   around the stars, silent at once,
where all the kites remind you to dream

and orchids go in rotund dances,
   a bright romance in all its riches,
giving the wind its perfumed glances,
   those beautiful eye-biting witches

   with costumes on all the songbirds,
with garters all over the lea,
   the seals are sleeping like tubas,
there are candles in all of the trees

and brides in gowns of snow,
   in their moment of beautiful curls,
in the Candle Grove take photos
   as the twilight sings out in the world

and the clock chimes on in the center
with the weight of a lover's tears
round the quiet of those playing checkers
with the bottle caps of their beers

as the acrobats stroll at their leisure
by the pond on their day off
where the only tumbles are breezes
and the music of sorrow is soft....

Let love bloom but let the heart go
and violets make time over it
for who needs a heart neatly broke
or the dreams of minikin bits?

For here is a park of beautiful things
for the world that comes to an end,
so all that comes to nothing sings
fulgent requiems

for in the graves next door, lovely as Hell,
beneath the elegant snip of the lawn
the skeletons yearn our elephant bells,
the Weltschmerz that is gone.

At twelve and eight (and don't be late)
the park has Bedlam parades
for the Night that is doomed from the top to the worms
and the Day of the Rising from Graves

for all that is hopeless is perfect, a dream,
let me living that dream be benighted
if the oranges taste so sharp they seem
beautifully unrequited.

Valentine for Moss Piglet

You are my yummy tardigrade,
my puffy little pet,
my water bear, my marmalade,
my sweet moss piglet.

I love you even chubbier
than water bears can get.
No one was ever lovelier
or more affectionate.

You laugh like a candied yam,
so cute and ticklish!
What you want is what I am,
what you like is what I wish.

For love and nothing more
I'd overturn a car
if I thought that you were bored
with parks and stores and bars.

If staying home instead,
after I wash the dishes,
we'd cuddle into bed
like two warm knishes.

I'd hug you through your belt loops,
I'd nibble your pecans.
I'd give you giant scoops
of kisses where you want.

I'd be your woolly socks
if your feet got cold.
My poems close Fort Knox
because you're the only gold.

You are my scrummy tardigrade,
my funny little pet,
my water bear, my lemonade,
my sweet moss piglet.

The Descent of the Water Palace

We were huddled in the door
by a tumbled downpour,
a closed umbrella shop
in the rain that wouldn't stop

when I saw you start to cry
where a parade should pass us by
and I tried my best to soothe
the requiem of truth:

This is not the rain, my sweet,
nor is it puddles at your feet:
the clouds made you a droplet dress,
that befits their true princess.

They brought you a silver gown
in a rush sweeping down.
To shame the thunder, brought to you
little gray ballroom shoes

for you, my love, are so dear
and like my heart they pour out tears
so big, so grand and so deep
it's only made from all we weep

and so we have the great parade
where all the watercourses played,
one that does not march the street
but falls like stars fast and fleet;

it's certainly not the rain, my love,
that wrecked the afternoon above
but one by one, from each chalice,
descends all day your water palace.

Pavan of the Yellow Curtains
(for Lou)

Fire is a dwelling-place
  I live in loving you,
there's no more beautiful face
  that light can wish to do.
Your kiss is fire's flakes
  from lips that burn me through,
there's no more lovely ache
  that heat can dream to do.
Your curve taught Undulate
  to a flame that thought it knew,
unchained in Conflagrate
  torrid exultant doom.
I long have lost my element,
  Love has changed me so,
I'm only a golden filament
  for the lightning you compose
lost in the ardent center
  no proof from burning knows
where the diamond begs for water
  and no salamander goes.

The Moon with the Daffodil Stars

Summer is the secret Heaven youth disclosed.
The moon with the daffodil stars settles with light and joy
like the ketchup spot crescent on lilac-scented clothes
of romping girls the chases with the run of laughing boys

whose globe requires nothing but kittens in knapsacks,
the wings to fly them always who are small as french fries
beyond the edge of hearing their parents calling them back
where begins the land of phantoms, buttercups and fireflies.

Silver is a promise that Gold is somewhere good,
the moon will help us find what the sun makes sweet by day,
and follows where they run and jump in their favorite wood

throwing rocks at the moon as hard as they may
to test how strong they are, how dreaming far away.
I'm sure he'd catch them were there any hope he could.

Illusion is the Mustache of the Heart

Love is a Spanish Magician
  that disappeared before my eyes
with a trill soft and patrician
  where our dreams were mesmerized.

Between the fire and the shadows,
  the sad and comic interludes,
he pulled from his hat with a *Presto*
  a bill for rabbit food.

Where the world is more than it could be
  I had such faith in its delights.
The show ended at 9:30
  but I hid there til midnight

when I crept into his dressing-room
  in the hope that I could find
the cape with the yellow runes
  and the power of Paradise

but all that was left of his costume
  was a mustache and bottle of dye,
a pair of worn out shoes
  and the sparkles of his eyes.

The Hospice on Tangerine Lane

Dying happens during the regular hours
  to strangers who are so far away
  it's meaningless in our heyday
down the street. Today is ours.

We do not have God's lonely powers
  to help our loved ones, to stave, to defy
  the end of love. We may powerlessly cry
in the same silent language of the flowers.

Some will argue that love lasts forever,
  that our memory is enduring, vital and true
    and, of course, it is not up to me to say

but I am living in that lost, foregone hour
  in the last when I'm about to lose you
    and everything I love will pass away.

Midnight at the Cathedral of Rabbits

No one that saw the snow squall round the church
wanted to sing, joke, drink or fall in love:
   the little white stars on the backs
   of five hundred rabbits, all of them black,
and the beauty of being cold, was enough.

Sunshine at The Spotted Albergo

The pool is closed for repairs.
  Down the elevator shaft
  another porter's cut in half
so everyone has to take the stairs.

The lounge is empty, the Ballroom sad,
  the web reviews are wroth and grim,
  the walls are slimy, the décor is dim,
daisies cover the helipad.

Ceiling mold forms a *trompe l'oeil*
  of cold phantasmagoric black
  as the sullen Grandeur turns its back
like the Hadean women of Hammershøi.

The central Fountain's *Dea Nutrix*
  folds on her crumbled pedestal,
  is now a landmark used to tell
the way to the town's VD Clinics.

Once the favorite of the Kaiser,
  the hotel where treaties were signed,
  where Michelin chefs came to dine,
is now the Paradise of misers;

how moguls and models would lustrous come!
  Beset these days by movie studios
  who save on set design for shows
about haunted houses or asylums

while a grisly police investigation
  of a prostitute dismembered
  is all your kids will remember
for all you've spent on your vacation

which, of course, is happening across the hall
  while in your room, red blocks of paint
  make banausic gestures to hide the faint
blood spatter on your walls.

The maids are from some Hell deployed
  to ignore all Do Not Disturbs.
  Grandmother's still dead at the curb
awaiting the notice of a bellboy

and the manager has horrible burns
  for reasons not entirely clear
  but across the police tape every year
we're shaking hands on my return

when the autumn leaves fall bright and fast
  and the sunshine's bald illumination
  makes the albergo look like a Dalmatian
laughing in the fire, rolling in the grass.

Sottosopra

The light was long and the day was hot
  in a January desperate to be cold.
  The sad, muscular snowblowers all unsold
shined at forty percent off in the lot.

Migratory birds chattered leafless treetops,
  daisies swarmed the sledding hill.
  Teachers longed for snow days, as they will,
and Mrs. Jennings, newly tenured, got shot.

The days go on and the lovers bloom
in the same clockwork and human doom
  assured, for all their dreams, it falls apart;

Only poets, malaria and the Monarchs of Hell
flurry in the upside-down and pell-mell
  dawn zeitgeber of broken hearts.

The Cancellation of the Plum City Phillumenists' Convention

It has to rain to make the Beauty of the world.
Some people have to have a really bad day
and we'll have to stay inside or catch a cold.

Water flooded the venue and I'm told
The Director and the food were washed away.
It has to rain to make the Beauty of the world.

Poor Cedric has a matchsafe made of gold
he's waited since September to display
but we'll have to stay inside or catch a cold.

Wren makes Jell-O coffins in a mold
when I suggested crafts like macramé.
It has to rain to make the Beauty of the world.

The umbrella sits in the corner like a scold
but it's no good when it's blowing sideways
so we'll have to stay inside or catch a cold.

Why do we get pneumonia or grow old?
Apparently, it's the only way.
It has to rain to make the Beauty of the world
and we'll have to stay inside or catch a cold.

The Horrible Sternutation of Mr. Gent

Your paperwork's all in order, I suppose,
bring this requisition down to Brent
and tell him the tickle factor of the nose
should be a simple-7 irritant

but unfortunately for Mr. Gent that day
an error listed B-13 instead
the kind of sneeze, unsupervised, that may
blow your sticky brains out of your head

and so, driving on a warm and sunny day,
the pollen index low and no ragweed,
he sneezed his sticky brains into his ashtray
and went marauding down the city street

for which Brent was reprimanded most severely,
written up and suspended (but with pay)
and punished so, Brent took his wife quite nearly
every morning to a matinée

while Mr. Gent was giving up his soul
and enjoying an awful barrel roll,
flopping around on fire out of control,
until he and his cruller hit a telephone pole

and were ejected through the windshield of his car
where he died outside of *Splash*, a topless bar.

The Orangery at the Dimpton Pleasure Garden
(to be completed in Spring, 2029)

When testing the new Moccasin-10 missile,
  alas, a hiccup is all it takes
  to shoot a barrage of awful mistakes
into piles of burning bones and crackling gristle

who, a minute ago, were drinking at the Pig & Thistle
  singing patriotic songs, wenching away heartbreak,
  a blast that bloomed their brains like angry cake
and flattened the land of sods and merrywhistles.

Sometimes the best and happiest lives
who are good to children and love their wives
  must be sacrificed for civil defense

so if a few irredeemable libertines
and poets are blown to smithereens
  it's certainly worth the cover-up and expense.

The Tormenting Trailers of Ferry Filbert

He was a deranged hermaphrodite who heard trailers
in his head...
O no, not now, please!
He liked his crazy hard... just like his sleaze!
Where's my medicine... just kill me instead!

He was a cat-fondling nudist on the sex offenders' list...
I'm not listening!
He shot himself in his panties at Buddy's christening....
And yet I'm still alive? *... and missed!*

He's a grizzled ex-pedophile... living on the edge...
Dammit, I am not!
Sorry... he's still a pedophile and likes his boys red hot!
I'm suing! *...it was alleged.*

Knock it off, you stupid assholes!
His face was imprinted in every cowboy's ass...
What??! *Wrestling with a secret from his perverted past...*
O come on! *See the shocking tale called... Beef Patrol!*

He was a bedwetter completely out of control...
That's it, I can't take it any more!
Who was this confused slob bleeding all over the floor?
Thrill to the tragic scandal in ... Chubby Roll!

The Night Castle of the Crocodiles

I wasn't as tall as the turnstiles
  but in my pyjamas was taking the tour
  that only happens midnight to four
at the Night Castle of Crocodiles.

In the hallway canals on left and right
  they rolled over and over at their feast
  of antelopes, zebras, wildebeests,
so I held my stuffed animals tight.

Normally dreaming at that hour,
I thrilled to the monsters, trumpets and towers
  and was buying some pencils in the gift shop

when everything suddenly flashed to a stop
with screaming, trampling, the shout of the cops
  because Miriam got herself devoured.

Our Top Story from *The Conspicuous Minister*

Local boob, seen here in an undated photo, met a gruesome and, some say, fellatious end....

June 28th — The wholesome delights of a perfect summer day at Requiem Beach were sodomized yesterday when unmarried part-time speed bump tester Fran Gardy ran himself over with his own jet ski exactly eight seconds after putting it in the water. Horrified witnesses reported seeing the forty-nine-year-old Gardy burst from the slip at launch speeds of 400 miles per hour, screaming away from the shore for about 350 yards before he flipped over the handlebars of the craft and swallowed his own jet ski, after which he promptly exploded. Maritime Recovery teams towed in parts of the fiberglass husk of his Yamaha 6000x *Cacafuego* in addition to Gardy's three-and-a-half inch penis. Soon after, the shock and sadness of beachgoers quickly turned to violence when local authorities tried to close the beach to conduct an investigation. An incensed crowd began by setting fire to Vanilla Plump's Ice Cream Shoppe then rampaged through parking lot B smashing car windows and pushing cars down the beach into the water before upwards of thirty rioters were shot by police. Outraged nudist Karl Creamie expressed a disgust shared by all the survivors: "I don't know why we have to lose a perfect day at the beach every time some ridiculous asshole recreationally explodes! I think the taxpayers deserve better than a police force constantly flying off the handle, a beach littered with dead children and grandmothers and some pointless investigation that closes a public retreat just because some imbecile decides to give a Yamaha a blowjob at 400 miles per hour. They found his penis, what else is there to investigate?!"

Authorities say the beach will remain closed for the next two months at a minimum to conduct the pointless investigation, until dead grandmothers are collected, all boardwalk shops that caught fire are rebuilt to standards and every automobile is dredged from the beautiful sea.

There Are First Days & Last Days

After I was fired from Factory 12 of Shubbie's Whipped Fluffy Cake Company for getting my underwear tangled in the Crème-o-tron, I somehow landed a job with Burl Flowers' Delivery Express. It was my first day on the job, 9:03 AM, my first house, when I knocked on the door in my crisp new uniform and it was answered by a five-year-old girl and her chihuahua.

Her chihuahua had been genetically modified to be eight feet tall, eleven feet wide and 983 pounds. The dog never barked but, apparently, in some secret government kennel, he had been taught English and was now mouthing through the storm door, *I am going to fucking kill you.* I decided to speak to the little girl instead.

–♪ Hi, what's your name? ♪

–Pumpkin.

–♪ Hi, Pumpkin! ♪ Your dog is mentally ill. I need you to keep this door *closed. Do not open this door* for any reason, under any circumstances, ok? I need you to hold this door closed with the strength of Jesus Christ. I am going to put my package down and then I am going to run away, screaming, back to my truck. Do you understand, Pumpkin?

–Uh-huh.

–Can you repeat back to me what I just said?

–Mmmmmmmmmmm……. You said that you and Jesus Christ are mentally ill for my dog.

–That's great, that wasn't even close, this is very important!

I didn't get two steps off the stoop when all of the sudden I heard:

–Pickles, no!!
–ROWWWWWWWWWWRRRRRRRRRRRRRRR!!!!!!!

The dog wasn't really biting me as much as he was merely hate-fucking me. I don't know how he got me out of my hot fleece jumpsuit but I do distinctly remember at one point using my bloomers as a tourniquet. Even though I was being fisted, what really irritated me was about *ten minutes* into this Animal Planet gangbang, Pumpkin leaned out of the door and said,

–The dog got out!

Your chihuahua is somehow using me as my own dildo, I'm very aware your dog is no longer with you, thanks a lot now. How about doing something actually useful, Pumpkin Obvious, like, I don't know, calling an ambulance, a priest, Animal Control, Dr. Ruth Westheimer, any one of these four people would be infinitely more helpful than you giving me periodic reports like:

–Mr. Man, your asshole's in my driveway!

You know how, when you're in your office – naked, semi-conscious and trying to cover your genitals with an Excel spreadsheet – your boss can magically no longer understand a word you're saying? It's annoying, isn't it? I clawed my way back nude to Burl's and simply asked Carol if the boss was in but she just sat there ignoring all the telephones and rudely hyperventilating

(I wonder how you get *that* job?) so rather than just standing there marveling at each other's naked disgust, I just walked into Mr. Flowers' office.

–Hello, Sir, we haven't formally met and I know you weren't expecting to have *this* conversation when you woke up this morning *but* even though it looks like I was giving a chihuahua a blowjob and a high-five, I wasn't having sex with animals, the animals were having sex with me. I also have to strenuously object to being yelled at by the motor pool manager: even though I was clinging to the truck to survive, I shouldn't be held responsible for bringing that same truck back to the office covered in dog orgasm, we don't have a hose at this operation? Really? Question: When does health insurance kick in for new employees?

–90 days.

–What about for sodomized employees?

–Sir, you no longer work here!

–What?? Why not?!

–Did you just ask me, Why Not? Did you really just ask me that?!

–Mmmmmmm...

–You're sitting in my office naked! There's jizm all the way to the elevator! Your prolapsed anus is ruining all of my furniture and you're telling me you fucked a chihuahua while sitting here in a Microsoft loincloth! A report, I hasten to add, that I have to present in two minutes!!

–Sir, some of those are valid points and I thank you for introducing them. I just want to jump in here and note that your report is on the non-penis side of my bikini bottoms...

–You idiot! Get out of here!

Being fired nude is upsetting, I am not trying to downplay that for those who've had the experience, but what's truly demoralizing, I think, is being fired by 10:23 AM. Walking home when the first stay-at-home mothers are just getting out to do some mall shopping and the sun still seems to have that sickly dawn feeling can really prick a person's morale, especially when you realize that the Price is Right isn't on for another forty-five minutes, a dignity marker I have sadly all too often sunk below. Your lunch is three hours away from reasonably being eaten and mocks you from the kitchen table for the effort. And if you're living with someone, there's the added agony that comes with the horrified Inquisition from a person who, not expecting anyone for another eight hours, erupts with stunned hysterics after thinking that someone is breaking into the house.

–What are you doing home??

–Other than the fact that I live here?

–Why aren't you at work?! And where are all of your clothes?!

–Look, I have had a rough day and I'm not in the mood to discuss at this very moment which one of us is nude and not at work at the company he somehow no longer works for...

–A rough day? It’s 10:30 AM, you woke up three hours ago!

–You know what, it’s really complicated and I don’t have the spiritual fortitude *right this second* to talk about the vagaries of fate and why I’m limping, flaccid and wet. I just want to lie face down on the floor and take *ten minutes* to decompress and massage my prostate!

–I’m just trying to understand why I’m looking at your genitals and we won’t have a paycheck this week!

–Alright, well, you know how chihuahuas get beefed up through government programs until their libidos unhinge and they go around raping everybody in the very natural, evolutionary enmity that has formed between delivery people and dogs?

–No! No, I do not!

–Ok, then I don’t see the point in going forward with this, honestly! It's like you've never seen a chihuahua before! Can you just do me a favor *this one time* and get me some ice cream and a towel, for God’s sakes!

The ordeal, of course, ends with a last, sardonic insult: three weeks later there arrives in the mail your first and last paycheck for $6.48, after the same chihuahua-mind-scrambling government takes out taxes. The mailman, who has not had sex with animals and will finish the day with a pension, delivers it to you shaking his head in disgust after a Union letter to all Deliveryperson chapters includes a graphic, salacious and grossly exaggerated account of the orgy, alongside your photo.

In any case, I’m not too worried about the future: I have an interview next Tuesday with Bob Crispy's Wild Time Chimp Experience and Primate Enclosure.

Schnapsidee at the Starfish Lounge

On afternoons like this, he seemed a decent sort:
he drank like a slob without falling down,
he bought us all our fair share of rounds
and laughed like a puppy confused by its snort

which made *you* laugh when life came up short.
An affable blimp disaster of a clown
who worked so hard to gang and horse around,
you knew his heart was down a couple quarts

so when he got caught in a murder-for-hire scheme
for three hundred dollars to kill a doctor's wife
to quash a costly divorce after an affair

the whole cockeyed, sordid mess just seems
to show all that's sad and desperate about life
til we realized we really just don't care

Patmos

After losing my Spirit, I am left with my personhood,
  something grounded in the world, in the creature,
  observable in its behavior, impelled by its nature.
Faith in the impossible is the desperation of the good.

I can never truly reconcile the balance
  between our tenderness, connection and charity
  and the ferality, vulgarity, depravity
that seems together to be one doomed inheritance.

I do not have the heart, the mind or the scope
  to understand our virtues or where our best
overrules our worst, where suffering to me is so terrible.

One can dismiss a whole pursuit as blind and cynical
  if unable to descend the desperate stakes of the jest
that are the same for the loving and the misanthrope.

The Chthonic Demotion of Malfeasance Mary Guttergung

We are an institution of terror,
of hate, perversion and utter misery.
Yet, I'm not happy that I'm grossly unhappy:
How do you *misplace* a covey of lechers?

The process is almost infernally easy:
You escort them to the Sixteenth Spirit, Zepar,
who locks them in a dirty pissoir
then you dump them in the cesspit of the sleazy.

Figure 33.
The Seal of Zepar.

What's here that actually confuses you?
The torture profile's neatly prepared,
the personal survey is designed for despair,
they're perfectly brutalized! There's nothing for you to do!

Mr. Guttergung, having tentacles is no excuse
nor is a love of sonnets, puppies or chloroform
that makes you prone to screwing up the forms
since all the options on the paperwork are Abuse!

And how exactly do you authorize an Early Release form
since we don't actually have one of those?
Spare me tales about your headaches and imperforate assholes,
because of you, I now have to send a Swarm

to Florida, of all disgusting places, which is why
we'll enjoy pulling out all your eyes.

The Window Washers

Well, screaming isn't going to help much, Love,
twenty-seven storeys in the air
and I couldn't recommend a whole lot of
crying, wriggling, bargaining or prayer,

I've dangled from a scaffold many times before
upside down like this and in a sway
even once back in 1984
right through the whole Thanksgiving holiday.

I once saw a skinnier man than you
separate from his leg at the socket
and I waited through the night to be rescued
all alone but for the birds eating it.

Of course, I don't mean to be so gruesome
I just like the new guys to be informed and chaperoned.
So, if we go, I hope it's as a twosome,
I'm tired of having to do this thing alone.

I've always thought if you don't land on your face
it will all happen much too fast to process,
the pain in direct proportion, in any case,
to the wind, the distance, your sins and the mess.

No, they won't be able to get a ladder way up here,
they'll probably have to rappel down to us.
I hope they send us some real mountaineers,
not Tim again, that hippopotamus.

Whatever you do, try not to shit your pants,
you don't want that in your face and hair,
if we survive, the press will take every chance
to get your picture in the evening fare.

We just got a whole lot of waiting now
bouncing off the building in the wind
getting to know each other somehow
before the dread hallucinations begin.

I'm glad to do the talking if you like,
believe me, I don't mind conducting,
I know too well about you silent types —
unless it's the rope around your neck obstructing.

I don't know why life goes hot and cold,
and how can I know what constitutes bliss?
But you can't find the beauty of the world
unless hung upside down above the polis.

When I see someone as unfortunate as you,
swarthy, clumsy, eternally forlorn,
boring in the way one is with a low IQ,
are you a Mars in retrograde Capricorn

or, more succinctly, do you like motorsports?
Who is your favorite pornographic actress?
Or actor, I'm for all kinds, of course,
when we hit the ground, we're all the same, I guess

and THERE WE GO! O HELL! That's really sad,
a little dim but he seemed like a good soul
but if he keeps drifting right just a tad
I wonder if he goes through that open manhole....

Start Your Own Witness Protection Program...

Just Like the Big Guys!

Even If You've Never Been a Witness Before!

Great for:

- **The Fatally Embarrassed (When it's your fault because it's your fault)**
- **Dull People (Why live as Douglas Snooze when you can be Trapezius Lazerforce McCannons?!)**
- **The Divorced (Child Support? Why, Trap McCannons isn't on *that* birth certificate!)**
- **Ex-Cryptids (Were you discovered by a fat, disgusting slob?)**
- **Housewives, Strippers, Morons and more!**

Blind? Concussed? Hallucinating? No Problem! You can still be a witness!*

Call for your New, Life-Changing Identity Kit Today!

False Witness, Inc. (631) 555-0009

**Poets not eligible for the program at this time.*

Bright as the Primrose Lightning

I'd love to make a spectacle with you,
something that you don't see every day,
I just need five hundred dollars to see us through.

Something so heedless between us two,
the building gets surrounded by Green Berets.
I'd love to make a spectacle with you.

Something Furor would play on kazoo
bright as the primrose lightning plays,
I just need five hundred dollars to see us through.

Something so grand it wouldn't do
at the office, on the bus, on Gallows' Day.
I'd love to make a spectacle with you.

Anything the stock exchange would rue
til the Bears and Bulls are little tears that say
I just need five hundred dollars to see us through.

We could make international news
despite everything that happens in a day.
I'd love to make a spectacle with you,
I just need five hundred dollars to see us through.

The Band with the Orange Plumes

The notes like apples and doughnuts
floated into our room.
We watched by the sunny window
the shakos with orange plumes.

The tumblers led them jocund from
the Dales of Perfidy
past the *Furniture Shoppe* of Plum's
who put his sofas on the street

where the crowd dazily reclined
with just the socks on their feet
while the tubas like rhinos tried
to make their heavy minstrels sweet.

The parade of Love was bright
with the music of dreaming youth
while a little child cried
for his melting Berry Smooth.

The teens were holding hands
and the veterans were weeping,
in the pet shop grass
dogs were huddled down and sleeping,

the food truck vendors for prime spots
were crashing and disputing
while the boy in polka-dots
was in his sister's arms saluting,

the college kids were marching drunk
in stumbles alongside
til four were trampled up
and one had nearly died

for which the crowd was laughing grandly
and dragged him to the curb
while the band played on so handy
with the beauty of the world

and only Time was missing
from the pomp and joy and fray
like a boy shy by his lisping
of the kissing he can't say,

or the poem on my desk
scratched out in its doom.
Our cuddle will never forget
the band with orange plumes.

The Graveyard of the Happy Love Poems

Here, the Ghosts and ashes do not stir,
  the silence twinkles in the cold, bare Tree.
  The voluptuous monument to Ecstasy
is crowned in endless twilight with black birds.

In Her giving hands opens the register
  of all who were sweet and simple and happy,
  who never cared at all what was to be
or that the truth was sadder than they were.

In this heavy, disconsolate still and gloom
  poems sleep like leaves that no one cares to read,
black and white in self-content, they fabulously bloom
  and sing to their own season, spin at their own speed,
leaving wit and art for their better lovers' doom
  whose dying is a hotter human need.

Winter of the Habitués

To escape the wind-gloomy, winter-haunted Creaks
   of a lonely old house, dark and remote,
   in a lopsided lawn chair, in my red peacoat,
I huddled to the snow with a drink.

It's lovely to watch through the twinkling bleak,
   the skaters circle, the flying iceboats,
   when you let the heart go like all asymptotes,
in love still with the curves you'll never reach.

Drinking myself into frostbite,
the snow falling softly through the night,
   I suddenly hear from a mile away

someone practicing a violin,
a request we welcome to join in
   the winter of the habitués.

The Balloonist of Whimsy Flats

Even a breeze has a little frontier.
  It wanders happily in its stream,
through the trees, easy and clear,
  unlike a Balloonist and his dreams,
the spiral descent of an aerostat
in the town of Whimsy Flats.

Why must such alighting dreams
  end tangled in telephone wires
while Engine Nine and rescue teams
  put out my gondola fires,
photographed upside-down
in every paper throughout town?

My off little hopes gazing up
  like goggled fools with tattered sails
are brought to ground in cold handcuffs
  and a booking at county jail
after the crowd asked Officer Brown
if they, this once, can shoot me down.

When did I start falling from the sky?
  I must have had the raw bad luck
absentmindedly walking by
  to not be seen by God and struck
by rebellious angels cast to ground
right on my head that knocked me down.

Other Balloonists are flying past
  and catching all the clouds in flight,
some with sweethearts, some with friends,
  through the diamonds of the Night.
Tears are funny, lonely and cheap,
shaped like balloons that sink to the deep.

A Letter from the Infernal Office of Lunatic Fancies

Todeskampf Office 11
46 Apricot Summer Road
The Finishing Meadow, Pickling, Hell

Dear Mrs. Wuenschel,

I hope this letter still finds you well. It has come to our attention that a Welcome Kit was sent to you from this office ahead of your actual Decease date and we are writing to inform you of the steps we are taking to resolve the matter. It seems a processing error caused by a clerk with tentacles reversed a date using the European convention in place of the American format required of your case, initiating the intake process a little ahead of schedule, and we most sincerely apologize for the confusion. We have corrected and refiled the paperwork, have resumed starving your specialists and assure you that all will be in order when you arrive. One or two staff members will also have their guts strewn all over the place.

Please disregard your Welcome Kit at this time, another will be provided soon to introduce you to the proper program and acquaint you with all that is due to you. Please accept the enclosed gift of monogrammed *Lacrimosa* handkerchieves as a token of our especial regret. We apologize once again, and unreservedly.

While we are not at liberty to discuss your hopeless case in detail, we recommend that you resume your mall walking, you increase your consumption of leafy greens and, if nothing else, you seriously consider killing Sean. Thank you for all you have done and we look forward to working you.

With My Delectation,
Captain Earnest Butcher, ILF, PQC
Officer, Lunatic Fancies, Unpleasant Division

A Satyrion for Grossofello

If not your clothes, I still commend you on your choice of witch,
Love, Revenge, Glamour, and I also can enrich,
I gave Valentino fire, an heir to the Viscount,
and I can help a brick like you at quite a nice discount.

When I look at your face I see you have a lot of pressing needs.
If your heat and hope is gone and there's no apple in your seed,
the flower's scorched, the serpent's dead, the wilt is at the ivy,
though a crone, my satyrion will make you bloom and lively.

I know the living grave of persisting when alone
and all the things that must go in a proper satyrion
the humor, dreams and nightshade, the bitters and lilac,
the broken-hearted milk that thickens an aphrodisiac,

a rhino's horn, a tiger's tooth, a yellow jacket's stings,
marmalade, a young girl's braid, the butterfat of things
that cry and laugh and pray for all we would hide from God,
finished with a keepsake and the backbone of a frog

it all goes in the witching spin that bubbles on the fire
if not for Love, the Heartless One, than for His fool, Desire
who doesn't endure but knows quite sure the cost of every hour
and loves to gamble for the scramble Time and Love devours.

As youth gets lost and living ghosts unquilt the threads of time,
get tangled in the lonely nights banished behind their blinds,
up by dawn, done by ten who take their tea at four
a spotless, cozy house despite no one to do it for

they comb their hair, iron their clothes, rake the autumn leaves
but it's surely not a life at all that doesn't take its sleaze
for it's not enough sometimes to get by on peanut brittle
and clinically impossible to give yourself a tickle,

too sad to face the crowded park, the gala's *joie de vie,*
or eat an entire cake each day from Margaret's bakery,
too obvious to go by yourself to the cinema,
eat in restaurants alone or mill about in bars

so what's to do with a life that you cannot share,
the lonely acts that sing to sleep when no one else is there?
What makes a quiet patience also works the nightmare bellows
but in your crumbled heart I see that you already know.

It's not intended to treat, cure, diagnose or prevent disease
(I am required by my counsel to include this legalese)
It hasn't been evaluated by the FDA
but I think it would be best if you just drink It anyway —

think of all the faith you have in life's other supplements,
to throw your legs in the air or otherwise get bent,
you can settle for the little porridge that you had before
but don't you think that you deserve a life with something more?

All you've suffered, all you've dreamed, the promises of mirth,
Time's too short to give to each their birthright on this earth,
just know that all of this goes in a Resurrection cup,
whatever you choose just be sure to drink the whole thing up.

The Sightseers

High above on a Double-Decker bus
  one is endowed with a flying sense of Pride,
  the tall Monarch of the passersby,
as if the spires were given just to us

until a strange, demotic impetus
  threw a rod, we jumped a curb and flipped eleven times,
  thrown through a pet shop window in just my shoes and tie
until my shoes blew off in a final flatus.

Carried on a stretcher with dead labradoodle puppies,
extracted from a fish tank, wet with golden guppies,
  I tour the city's sewer plates and monuments' feet;

one doesn't get the true sense of a city's character
from public gardens, gold churches, ruined aquifers,
  that one does waiting for an ambulance in the street.

The Astronomer Rests By Lidget's Shieling

There is no Night so lost or too far
  I can't find my place in its distance
  despite its sometimes blank insistence
it's just a crown discarded in the dark.

All is quiet over my small song.
  I must believe in love's endless majesty
  but what if I find in its abyssal beauty
its stranded light, the light already gone?

Love has its own astronomy.
  How cold and vast it is but I,
for all its blind, precise mystery,
  still see a heart to hope and pilot by

though tonight it's the same sad story:
  locked out again from my Observatory
I'll head down to Credo Alvera's bar
  as it's only there that I can see the stars.

Once the Flower is for Someone Especially

Once the flower is for someone especially
  and enters the language of love and wish and time,
all is for the Night, the faith, the Beauty,
  in the back of a hearse or as a Valentine.

It tokens all our power for a day
  for all the rain that's been and all the fire
that's made itself so sweet, then dies away
  brute witness to the claims of our desire.

All the flower becomes of us imparts
  its passion to our troth, its defiant fragility,
its radix draws its temperance from the dark,
  its strength is in its mute humility
so even if it breaks just like a heart
  Love has its towers now along the sea.

The Lightning, Like Sodom's, Destroying and Gold

The Lightning, like Sodom's, destroying and gold,
all we were beautiful and all we have known,
the places we cuddled as the Sun went down;

our lives disappeared through the wild of light,
with the square, the meadow, the allée we biked
but still we are happy, in love, the Drowned.

Where there should be panic and fire brigades
all through the town are splendid parades
ringing black bells instead of alarms.

I'm running to you where the flames sweep away
half of the town in less than a day
covered in ashes to fall in your arms.

Colonel Velvet's Billiards and Grill

There's a place in the heart
  where pool hustlers gather
and girls who like bikers
  come in from their leather

and each Night repeats
  drink, money or love,
somebody cheats
  and it all kicks off

the pool cues are broken,
  the jukebox destroyed,
the girls' pepper spray
  is liberally employed

a kick in the nuts,
  a stick in the ass,
Sleaze Dog unconscious
  face down in the glass,

Nikolaj vomits
  and Sudsy cries,
I'm pretty sure Edbert
  slunk off to die

as Tim F. is thrown
  in the great Fireplace
and Gregg Buffleson
  is punched in the face

while two lovers dance,
  covered in beer,
to Chico's screaming,
  stabbed in the ear

while off in the corner
  writing his book
a poet oblivious
  to the whole donnybrook

lost in memories,
  dreams and cares
he and his Muses
  are hit with a chair

his great inspiration
  hid under the table
then ran far away
  as fast as was able

passing Jack in the door
  smiling away
after pissing the wall
  his big sobriquet

when Woodmont suffers
  an awful barrage
that no hope can save
  and no love triage

then the kitchen is closed
  as Cookie is dead
though Stu gets the special
  right in the head

then bounces off Caro
  onto his back,
who's then trampled by
  the big lumberjacks

as poor Anton's head,
  agog and in gore,
bumps into Stu
  then rolls round the floor

round a flurry of fists,
  clobbers and clouts,
by four set on fire
  that no one puts out

as the owner's picture
  of his mother and him
breaks over the head
  of Matricide Jim

and Trixie's husband
  comes in for his wife
and all of her lovers
  run for their life

then from the bar
  a shotgun appears
and breaks with its warning
  the heart's chandelier

til it finally ends
  at its crescendo
and Crushie is tossed
  right through the window

and everyone's tired,
  bloody and flattened,
we come to the bar
  like nothing has happened

as if nothing occurs
  in the world outside
and all is at peace
  in our moment of quiet

though all the girls
  on the corner of Vine
in their short skirts
  shiver all Night,

disappear one by one
  midnight to five
lost in the cars
  that come creeping by

so all goes the heart
  both restless and still
to the flickering light
  of the Billiards and Grill

while the moonlight shy
  peeks at the window
and lightly, in tides,
  it starts to snow.

The Pickle Villa By The Sea

In a little place in which you know
you cannot stay for ever,
                    the beach towels swaying on the line,
where the clouds are just the vanishing caps
of a calendar of cigarettes,
                    the *nefasti* of olives and a glass of wine,

it's nice to leave a dream in the stratigraphy.
Cherished things live in blesséd proportion
                    to their brute survival in our memory
even as the short glamour says
long after it's far too late
                    Look at the timeless beauty of the sea.

The Misfortune that is sure to come
may already have left Its seashells at my feet,
                    the slippers of His tumbled retinue,
but It cannot crash Its tides on this cocktail
nor disturb my afternoon's purple pail
                    where I collected a few tumbled ones for you.

Ice cubes folding in a summer glass
make an audible wink under the blankets of the heat.
                    Joy and Sadness here have no propitiation,
they are hot together and from their depth rejoice
like the garland above the Gate of Nowhere's voice
                    through the darkness of the only initiation

into this grateful moment we can achieve
that bids us welcome as it bids us leave.

~

I nap in a chair, I listen to the garden,
I read some obscene little poems,
        a little lonely that I have nothing else to do.
Peace that is part dragon and part lion
Its wings drive the gentle breeze into the impulse
        to cut my heart in half with vermouth.

Uriah

To be set in the hottest part of the battle
near to the wall where the archers
throw their murder volley from the sun
while holding on desperately to my strength
in the shouting, dying zigzag of confusion,
the terrible violence of our barest center
killing everything all around me
even as I pressed forward in the crush
only to see a band of valiant men
slowly approach to set themselves upon me,
their tawny hunting dogs on a chain
who I briefly saw in my imagination
curled together quiet around a hearth
until I was awakened by the cold sense
that I am far away
emerging from the finish of a wave
when I turned around and saw
Joab and all his men, all my own,
stare like thieves at me as they withdraw

now laying here hacked to pieces
a corpse on my left and the trunk of a man
I cannot reach crying on my right
I can finally see the summer
the quiet bright blue, the ice cream shop light
that shines over the joy and freedom of children,
over the young men and the young women
meeting in the spray of a fountain
the prisms dripping from their perfumed hair
where the *passeggiata* is driven like a breeze
only by its own neighborly delight
as I lay here in the time when kings go to war
spattered again and again with blood

like a flower in the rainy field

in sleepiness...

how my wife is now so far beyond me

how the summer is going everywhere without me

how this sun is so beautiful and intense

look how we're curled together around its hearth.

Doubloon

Doubloon is an old rodeo clown
  with a lasso of red macramé
but this is not a rodeo town
  and the train's not coming this way.

He can tell you how many sorrows he's drowned
  and how many times he was gored,
but the rodeo isn't coming to town
  and they don't take Doubloons at the store.

The only horns he fears are the cars
  shouting that he step aside
and he drags his red lasso into the bars
  where the liquor and bartender's snide,
and the mechanical bull's too big for his heart
  even at a quarter a ride.

An Invitation to an Abattoir

I have somehow done it yet again:
  the toilet overflowing across the floor,
  an impatient multitude outside the door
of soon-to-be horrified former friends.

I will need all my charm and powers for an excuse,
  ankle deep in merde and mortal doom,
  frantic to burn down *another* bathroom
or form designer towels into a noose.

The Aceldama of another perfect night
  that howls in panic and the poisoned air
  perhaps I'll say this slick was already there

  long before I innocently arrived?
  I drink all the shampoo but survive.
I open the door and pre-emptively start a fight.

Amusement for Peter Crepuscule

If Death is like a penny candy
  (I say *if* because we haven't met)
  I hope its cold, efflorescent mint
sweetens away my head.

Life lives like Red Hots on the tongue
  so just like its sizzle melts away,
  the funeral director leaves candy on a tray
exactly like Uncle William, who was young.

I hope to meet the Great Confectioner
  with His staff of honey and chocolate Aurochs
  but before you close the lid on my box
overshake my memory with sugar.

But if Death *is* most foul (I've seen some things)
  and spiteful pulls my feet up through my nose,
  the infinitude of Beauty is ours to compose
anyhow that's sweet; let the jellies sing.

Bal des Ardents

I don't know how or by whom it all started,
  the fire, the sprinklers, the bump into the wheelchair
  that bounced poor Prunella down the stairs
and landed on Mrs. Crumbs, who infarcted,
at least before Pru mortally departed
  she didn't blame me as, gasping for air
  from her crushed windpipe, she seemed to declare
her belief that Roger Crumbs did it, then she farted
  herself into a seizure and passed away.

Sadly, I guess, we'll never know,
  I was joking when I said to him, *Way to go...*
and he, lunging at me, went head-over-feet
  down the stairs, through the window and into the street
and that's his head over there in the driveway.

Tricoteuses in Sunflower Square

What a shame that one, and only seventeen.
  I'd do him on a dirty bathroom floor.
  I wish instead it was my brother-in-law,
his head just holds his drink, the Philistine.

Well, for what they're charging, I think it's obscene.
  What you kill an aristocracy for
  if you're going to pay high prices like before?
I almost stayed home rather than come to guillotine

though if I had to look one more minute at my Fred
  I'd have thrown that boy into this filthy mob
and made the Executioner lop off mine instead.
  No more my Robert, that aquatic slob —
ugh, here comes Celine...so she's escaped her cowshed.
  Wave. Well, I never thought I'd see a tomato sob,
isn't she brave, wearing all that red....

Our Top Story from *The Conspicuous Minister*

August 11th — Unmarried two-time PGA Champion Ron Factor shot 76 yesterday in the third round at the Tilbury Town Classic in what could only be described as the worst mass shooting in Golf history, this after reports that he shot 69 on Friday and 64 in an opening round so depraved, it included the senseless killing of four Eagles. Experts at this newspaper can only speculate upon what set off this savage rampage as no manifesto has been recovered as of this filing; leading theories range from a particularly bad mood to a diagnosis of CTE after years of reverse gangbangs with pornographic actresses. Former South African champion Johannes Roedens noted that Factor has been slicing into innocent crowds with alarming frequency ever since last year's cup win at Hardbostle and has recently added a hook to his swing that Roedens called "regrettable." When interviewing spectators about the murders, they all responded with baffled silence, clearly too shocked to process the outrageous slaughter they had witnessed throughout the tournament; the only thing we, the living, can do is reflect mournfully on the tragedy and pray that time will bring healing and comfort to all those who lost a loved one. This paper has made a strident appeal that all future Golf events be cancelled until the governing body for the sport can review and improve their safety procedures so that this atrocity never happens again. We stand with the victims' families to decry a sport so violent as to be criminal in its callousness and we will use all legal means to bring the executives of the sport to account.

A Magog at Vanilla Plump's Ice Cream Shoppe

I know you told me I have to mind my pressure
  and just let the little things slide off my back
  or else I'll have some kind of walrus heart attack
or be taken down by SWAT like Uncle Chester

and I promised to respect our wedding vows,
  knowing you could have married that millionaire,
  and to take, in my oath to love and care,
my anti-psychotics before I left the house

so I'm sorry to do this by voicemail
  but I am pretty sure I'm going off to jail,
and you're not getting your vanilla squares with pecans:

what started as a light dispute about coupons
  I've somehow turned into a hostage situation
that no longer is open to negotiation.

The Obituarist Ziplining at Muscatuck Mountain

In my profession, it's hard not to imagine
  a thousand spectacular things going wrong:
the teen ogling my wife forgets to strap me in
  and I land in the parking lot on a guy in a sarong;

the wire snaps in half and I drag the ground
  on my face and testes to my closed-coffin wake;
I scream or laugh and a bird flies in my mouth
  and I choke to death for adventure's sake;

they send another zip before I complete my run,
  and smashing into me, I'm fatally sodomized;
I stop halfway as the park closes for lunch
  until I'm devoured by vultures and horseflies;

I start bouncing and get tangled in the wire
  and hang myself in erotic asphyxiation;
or lightning strikes and I'm a flying fire
  and just my head goes to the finish station;

slingshot through an open window,
  killing four at a local junior high,
all are Obituarists below
  while overhead an obit passes by;
upside-down in my harness, how can I
be so in love with life, knowing what I know?

The Cute, Enraged Fluffle at Mrs. Groomer's Petting Zoo

Sometimes when Love, drink and poems,
when television will not do,
one wants to connect to their local beasts
at the petting zoo,

to pet a goat or rabbit
even to watch a squirrel
who's not part of the exhibits
run around that world,

where the day can go anywhere
if I believe it's true
despite my bills and errands
and all the work that's due

but if you've traveled with me at all
you know where this thing ends:
when life goes on all-fours,
I find life's human sense.

It starts with gentle petting
and ends at the hospital
with me prone and screaming
covered in animals.

Three dollars a tub got me
all the food I need.
It started with *I Love Animals*
and ended in stampede.

Nibbling from my hand
seemed to go all right
then one went off his head
and lunged in for a bite

then the whole fluffle erupted
with blind ferocity!
Please don't ask me how
they got in my cavity.

The security guard kept asking
to see my All Day Pass,
while an EMT was pulling
the rabbits from my ass.

Arthur Maggie's schoolchildren
formed a fevered queue
to get the civic lesson:
What Not to Be or Do.

I know that with rabbits
there are better ways to cuddle
and, No, Officer Brown,
they weren't being smuggled.

I remember at the Tiger Show
they balanced on a ball,
I was slightly disappointed
that the trainer wasn't mauled

so it's fitting I was naked
with kibble in my hair
as the horrible entertainment
in the sunny thoroughfare.

A priest was eating ice cream,
A husband comforts his wife,
the Fire Chief held my bloomers
while they used the Jaws of Life

and Aafaq Al-Salamah
from WKTU
was standing with a llama
conducting an interview

as the crowd titillated
how it went so wrong:
Was he picking up the rabbits?
Was he stringing them along?

Was it their natural instinct
to see his fat as prey?
Is it that he's so repellant?
Is it his unlucky day?

Did he put them in his underwear?
Was he juggling them for fun?
Did he startle them with a flatus
or annoy them with a pun?

Was he teasing or fondling them?
Or was it his cologne?
as I went from zoo to zoo
as a picture on each phone.

I apologize to my community
for what's corrupting, daft and gross,
that I'm always the wretched reason
that the rabbit hutch is closed

but life is a golden promise
despite how good we are
each day is the petting zoo
that sometimes breaks your heart.

The Psychopomp for Dovey Berg

When Fate awoke and filled Her water bowl
  to wash Her little hands before eating Her plums,
  on the sill, a songbird had succumbed
 to the unsuspecting temperature She made cold.

Being Fate, She cannot pity or cry,
  neither hurt in Her heart nor love in Her soul.
  She wears a white ribbon that is the scroll
of all the names today that are to die.

When *I* awoke, I cut myself shaving,
  burned my hand on the stove and fell down the stairs,
changed a tire in a puddle, cold and raving,
  only to find a nail in the spare
at the same time a Mack Truck was hydroplaning
  when I heard a songbird singing, unaware
I was heartened at the moment I was beyond saving.

The Double Dutch Slaughter of Sherbert Jones

Kamisha and Besinda love to play all day
while most kids like to jellyfish inside
(such that Play60 had to make PSAs
to beg these lazy assholes to go outside)

and today was expected to be like any other
with the thousand little tumults in the street,
the joyous billows of feeling, and Mabel's brother
crying for the chocolate ice cream at his feet.

How all was bright with song! How the laughter shone!
The sidewalk full of life, the afternoon with hope
for everything alive except for Sherbert Jones
who liked his joy with mold, like every misanthrope.

How he hated the summer which encourages such things,
the depraved happiness Sherbert just despised
that deserves a smash in the face but resolved its reckoning
to Sherbert rushing past with averted eyes.

How the jumping dancers leapt with speed and grace and touch
as the ropes swung around them like fast oscilloscopes
until Jones bumbled absently into their Double Dutch
and with his own nimble grace was strangled by the ropes.

He laid there on the pavement like a misconfigured slug,
as if the ropes had squeezed his paunch into his bloated head.
When they tried to untangle him, they stepped right on his nuts
whereby he shit his pants, and then Sherbert Jones was dead.

Besinda and Kamisha still love to play all day,
the sun shines on them both with golden glittering
and when misanthropes see them, they run the other way.
In the summer air these lovelies Double Dutch and sing:

You break your neck, you bust your bones
when you jump rope like Sherbert Jones.
You take a chance each time you dance
now Sherbert's dead and shit his pants.

Hey, whatcha doing? Hey, whatcha know?
Who's that fool with nuts up his nose?
I like jump rope and romance,
Sherbert's dead and shit his pants.

Mabel's brother is running home
to tell his momma he dropped his cone.
She'll slap him stupid, with both hands,
til dead like Jones and shits his pants.

Corrigendum from *The Conspicuous Minister*

August 13th — All of us here at *The Conspicuous Minister* apologize for the report published two days ago of a series of mass killings at the Tilbury Town Golf classic by two-time gangbanging PGA champion Ron Factor. After further research, an outraged public response and several lawsuits filed against us, we determined that the numbers reported were Factor's actual Golf scores and not body counts. Apparently, our new Golf correspondent has never heard of Golf and was unfamiliar with its basic rules, its scoring, commonsense and journalism. We have closed our sports desk for the foreseeable future and our editors have yet again assaulted all responsible.

The Conspicuous Minister regrets the error.

The Recidivists' Support Group of Lentil County
(*Meets in the Little Annex basement on Tuesdays at eight, with refreshments*)

I guess my outlook on Love is pretty grim
  but then there I am lonesome once again
  wandering Garland Park at 4:00 AM
in love's bunglesome recidivism

until my heart is nothing but a winter prism,
  a little crooked icicle in the night
  by which I chase each color of morning light
to another rumpled bed of her or him

and maybe I've just got the whole thing wrong,
like a fortifying tipple or happy song,
  and what I dream is all that's left of mine

but it seems now not a question of faith,
nor a coast between Life and Death
  but all alone to make my peace with time.

In the Sleek of the Sickly Wood

Beware you the lurk of *Lebensmude*,
in the Sleek of the Sickly Wood
down brambled ways, in the cold outskirts,
behind the Beautiful Park at Weltschmerz
where flowers are lovely but roots are foul
and the Glimmers of promise sink in the ground,
the dogs are out hunting your simplest dreams
and the birds of the Damning pick your bones clean,
the black steam rises from feverish ponds
where all the frogs are fat with Despond
and there are hyenas who howl with delight
whenever you're downtrod, lonely and slight,
how sharp at the fang is the bite and the laugh
at the hope and the valor that's bitten in half,
where all your ambition and all your best toil
will ooze into mire and pucker with boil,
youth will dull early and age will regret
the wishes to pay on the footpath of debt
over the bones who have faltered before
that clatter the wind and nothing more
while signs lead you every which way
in the wood's hunger to hold you to stay,
to feed its dark, and thicken its fog,
the Gloom that's glory for its heartsick God,
where Love has a portion and a crumbled estate
and lives with Its trophies until it's too late
to see Its way out and settles to bed
in the heart that goes dying its Land of the Dead,
and Beauty is there, in an Icicle Court,
who undoes her buttons as a last resort
as the mirror amative tells her to trust
what is noble in Love but truer for Lust,

Beware, Beware, O sweetheart, Beware
the wood of the slithers, the creeping Despair,
the dark without angles, the cry without center
where the Exit goes through the confusion of Enter
to the beasts so starving their ribs show through
where one of those ribs will soon be you
slain in the hunt and put on the dish
of Time in His Hall of *Too Far to Wish*
to feast on His partridge, get drunk on His wine,
to eat you with olives, apples and swine,
God help those that find that *Lebensmude,*
heavy and longing and destitute,
insane with the song that somewhere is good
in the Sleek of the Sickly Wood.

Limes in a Bedlam Crap House

Life eats its pickles and sighs.
It wants to be funny and sad
all at the very same time
and the Good runs off with the Bad

but I live like *P.Fumarii*
in the heat of my own little plume,
like a mouse that puts cheese on his belly
and makes yum sounds all afternoon

while the clock in the graveyard chimes
that time is too big and too small
in the Land of the eyes of the Twilight
for the darkness that's coming to all

but we still get our pudding on Tuesdays
and if Nurse sleeps well past Prime
after getting drunk at Compline
we all get wedges of lime

fresh from the town of Midnight
on napkins embroidered and pink,
I save them to lick in the moonlight
when I like to be quiet and think.

O! where is my teenage heartbeat
with its crisp of cucumber?
Where is the cool still sweet
through the sprinklers of August summer?

I'm called a vulgar little gloom,
a gruesome and pestilent cynic
who poisons everything good in the clinic,
even when laughing at doom!

In my room is a *Portait of Circus:*
Elephants on Bicycles
where the man at the popcorn stand
is especially tragical

who lives by a quarter a bag
and makes a dollar twenty five
and only his yearning for Brenda
keeps his sad little pickle alive

and the one that painted that Portrait
is yelling down Darkly Hall
that we're Limes in a Bedlam Crap House
and there's no way out at all.

There is no way out at all.
There is war, disease and famine,
greed and filth and madness
in the hearts where the waghalters call!

O! great is the King of Bedlam
with his retinue of Nightmares!
We are his footstool of Beauty,
the paupers of God's kind care!

Axis of June

The meadow of God's Greatness in my heart,
so free, so bright with life, and gold
in all His limitless power and His art,
the eternal beauty of being five-years-old,

in the same boundless play a friend of mine
threw a spear from the top of the slide
that hit me like a lightning in my eye.
My outrage thought on a response. Then I cried.

I ran home convinced I was blind,
a permanently deformed monster of Disgrace
and the blood running down my nose meant I was dying.
Of course, I got in trouble for getting hit in the face.

For the rest of the day, I had to stay inside
and I sat at the window with a patch on my eye.
As I heard the roaring summer on the slide
I felt my first measure of hopeless Time.

The Blue Pearmain

When I was lurking late down Christian Lane,
  after drinking my cups and fighting in my irons,
  I heard the sadness of the addicted Sirens
from the third floor window of the Blue Pearmain

where three Witches unfolded from the door
  sloth-eyed, toothless, tattoos on their faces
  of crosses, tears, children's names, enlacements
over the names of the pimp they had before.

What's human in the flesh never forgets
the first twined promise of Life and Death
  and in their dead despair, recognized me.

Suffering conforms the soul to Christ.
What else could I give you but human delights
  that lead where all human sorrow leads?

Mephistophelian Transposition

My critics jeer at my perfume of beer,
that my asshole's leading me wrong,
I'm quite out of touch and I fart so much
I mix up my wind with my songs,

Ah, but I laugh at their spasms of wrath,
for each has their *locus amoenus.*
As Life goes on despite what you want
why bother to wrestle my penis?

Not only my belly bulges like jelly,
my tail's too long to control,
it gets up one's dress and makes such a mess
uncoupling's a rigmarole

til a squeal and a feel that's a little too rude
is piquantly balanced, and perfectly nude.

Gomorrah of the Lyres

A poet, he was always insufferably doomed
and his house sat in the asshole of the town;
when helicopters crashed into his livingroom,
I was sure it was the Muses shot them down.

He was especially confused by Love and Death
but pinned down by a copter and on fire
rather than put his brains back in his head,
voiding his bowels, he was so inspired

by the metaphor of being chopped in two,
a Love poem in couplets would surely do
but as the poem was about to close
the fire department hit him with the hose.

Muses Insurance agreed to pay for the roof
but not to have the helicopters removed.

Ursine Industries Presents: A Berserker Tableau

Len Liske had been attacked by bears many times before. His first savage encounter was in the seventh grade during class picture day when a bear wandered into the gym and was immediately offended by the smell of the hair gel Len used to slick down his unruly cowlick (his mother bought two 8x10 and two wallet size action shots of the mauling in addition to an aftermath photo that sits on the family mantel to this day.) In subsequent years, Len was attacked by Black bears, Grizzly bears, and two Kodiak bears on an ill-informed trip to Alaska which was undertaken for the sole purpose of escaping bears; he was once victimized at the Neuberger Brothers' Dazzling Times Circus when he got up to go to the bathroom during the *Bears on a Unicycle* routine during which he not only suffered severe bites but was also beaten with unicycles. He has even been attacked by a woman dressed as a bear, an escaped mental patient from Besom House who had the florid hallucination that she was a bear whose crime-fighting mission was to defeat her arch-nemesis, Len Liske, despite Len's hysterical insistence that he has no idea what the Hell is going on. So when the neighborhood bear showed up at his niece's birthday party, standing on his hind legs at nine feet tall, Len decided to take prompt, pre-emptive action and walked right up to him and punched him in the guts. The bear, bewildered and insulted, just looked at Len incredulously — a mild-mannered animal who was there only to wish Len's niece a happy birthday and give her a gift of salmon was now just assaulted for no apparent reason. The bear, in a conciliatory gesture, decided to try and "hug it out" with Len but Len naturally saw this as just another vicious attack and the two quickly started trading punches, tumbling around the backyard locked in furious combat, crashing into the table with all the presents, destroying the cake and ultimately falling onto Aunt Selima who failed to notice the ruckus while absorbed in telling, for the hundredth time, her story about the time she dated famous Golf pro, Ron Factor, for two days back in 1986. When the police and Animal Control arrived, Len was booked downtown on charges of aggravated assault, animal cruelty, elder abuse, corrupting children and animals and public nudity. He is currently serving time in Pemberton Zoo in Greenland from which each year on his niece's birthday, Len sends a card expressing his regret that he cannot be with her to celebrate but sends his deepest love and affection. The bear attends every birthday party and also visits Len's niece on Christmas.

Trouvailles in the Blooms

Poor Terry, a tire tread on his chest,
his right leg in a tree across the road,
half his ass on his head while the rest
delights children in another postal code,

his headphones knotted around his penis
gave him a purple, deviant insouciancy
while his fart face frozen *in extremis*
bestowed, on the roses, a tender pity.

His nude and shattered person drew a crowd
half-horrified but perfectly entertained
where a bit of cheek raised a laughter loud
how Terry could have been so scatterbrained

but though all over the place, sad, daft and grim,
by suppertime we left (Hell if I was going to touch him.)

Piano for Mulberry Head

Pushing a piano down the street,
while veering to get a soda,
the cobbles under the piano's feet
made the bubbles of a coda

but the cop that tragically appeared,
who likes music with his Pernod,
made it quite arrestingly clear
the piano would have to go.

You cannot run that piano through town,
it's against all traffic laws
then just like that D-flat resounds
with a rude little guffaw.

I'll run you two in as fast as you like
and then we'll see what's funny
as the piano played *Music for Sprites,*
up tempo and in G.

No one's more sorry than I am,
Sir, this obstreperous piano
is causing such a traffic jam,
the way is hard and slow

and as I struggled through the square
how that damn piano played.
The cop roared with despair,
Are you trying to start a parade??

The streets are rough and he's ticklish, Sir,
but we'll try to go quiet and quick
for with a song in his heart and a weakness for liquor,
he tends to get lovesick

which is why I am trying to get him home
as you would a drinking piano.
It's certainly something I don't condone
but how he gets out, who knows?

And as you'd expect the music ends
with a minor altercation
and we were arrested once again
for public intoxication.

All through the night he played in our cell
Piano for Mulberry Head
for the love of drink, for the love of a girl,
with the heart of a sick little clef.

The Uxorious Disaster of Reggie Dribbles

I know I ruined your High English Tea
  and you just *hated* my birthday gift,
that I spoiled a perfect day on skis
  when I fell from the top of the lift,

that I mucked a perfectly harmless affair
  when I found you both under the covers,
that I should have taken reasonable care
  when I backed the car over your mother,

and people should just ignore me
  when I can't help being your Reggie,
whenever an animal gores me
  or I hang in the hall by my wedgie,

would you prefer I die on a Friday
  so you get off early from work
or will that just spoil the weekend
  and drive your mother berserk?

Would Tuesday be better, Darling,
  when nothing is going on?
Or is that the day you meet with friends
  for gossip and mah-jongg?

I know Sunday isn't proper at all
  as that is your day of rest.
I can't expect you to make any calls
  because you've had a death.

I was thinking that Monday is possibly nice?
  You're right, that's already bleak:
there's nothing like a dreary demise
  to set up the rest of the week.

I won't even mention Saturday night
  when you want to go out on the town
which would be so typically impolite
  to expect you to be homebound,

and I know that I am an utter disgrace
  for my boring, low-status job
and whenever you look at my paunch and my face
  you must drink with your friends or you'll sob.

Though Thursday is all of your favorite shows,
  would you consider the DVR?
I'm always troubling things, I know,
  even when crossing the bar.

I'll try my damnedest to go on Wednesday
  if you'd like me to pencil it in
and if I overshoot it, I'll ask
  someone to do me in

because, I'm sorry, I got so distracted
  trying to schedule the day,
by a bus I was bisected
  that was coming the other way.

Though I can't find my legs or my wallet,
  I'll call Sanitation tomorrow.
We can still dance at *The Mollusc.*
  At least I won't tread on your toes.

You, Too, Will Fall in Love

Among the Vespas circling the busy square
  around the Central *Fountain of the Sun*
  our best Messenger is certainly on one
from the Romantic Office of Lost Affairs

and though his briefcase flew into the air,
  was run over, scattered and horribly trampled on
  so that all the crucial paperwork is gone
we're sure our Messenger is almost there

with all the Seals and privileges of Fate
  as sanctioned by Hell and Heaven up above
and though time feels so lonely and so late
  you will for all disasters fall in love,
  for though the world always has enough,
by its Grace, each lover has to wait.

In the Pale Light of the Knacker's Yard

♫ O dogs, don't maul me again.
O dogs, don't maul me again,
though all my misdeeds are the knackeries
that have laid me down with the damned.

O rats, don't bite me again.
O rats, don't bite me again.
I've taken as much as any man can
alone to the bitterest end.

O crawlies, don't burrow again.
O crawlies, don't worm in again.
I know the worst get what they deserve
and I've given my best to them.

O bunnies and fluffy things, No.
O bunnies and fluffy things, No.
Please let the mice be Paradise nice
and the chipmunks leave me alone.

O cows, don't trample me flat.
O cows, don't trample me flat.
Covered in cud, mud and in blood,
it's hard to make money like that.

Fortune's my own Beldam,
Fortune's my fierce Beldam.
She comes for the rent I've already spent
with a broom in Her awful right hand.

My way is troubled and dark.
My way is troubled and dark.
Don't come to correct with Your stone on my neck,
with the weight of Your hand on my heart.

My heart is all stubbles and gorse.
My heart is all stubbles and gorse.
I could barely last week sit up and speak
kicked in the head by a horse.

All that I've suffered, I've earned.
All that I've suffered, I've earned.
I went out once in the beauteous evening
and my goodness never returned.

I am a witless buffoon,
a lickerous, witless buffoon.
The ideas of a fool go out with misrule
and come back like a typhoon.

I have felt what I lost all my dreams.
I have felt what I lost all my dreams.
Is there any kind place for a lost scapegrace
to find the peace that redeems?

O Life, don't hurt me again.
O Life, don't hurt me again.
But if coming to kill the hogget,
put the bolt from my heart in my head.

What makes a pale, cold light,
so pale and so cold a light?
On the sweeps of a dream sails Yesteryeen
and its postcard sinks through the Night.

I know it's the best for all that.
I know it's the best for all that.
I don't have the right to ask for respite
but it's all I have left, and my cat. ♪

www.ingramcontent.com/pod-product-compliance
Lightning Source LLC
Chambersburg PA
CBHW070247100426
42743CB00011B/2174
* 9 7 8 0 5 7 8 7 7 0 5 7 4 *